Copyright © 2015 Claire Arene-Ikedi

All rights reserved. No part of this publication may be reproduced, transmitted, or stored in any form or by any means without the prior written permission of the author and publisher.

All Scripture quotations, unless otherwise indicated, are taken from the Holy Bible, New International Version, NIV. Copyright © 1973, 1978, 1984, 2011 by Biblica, Inc ™ Used by permission of Zondervan. All rights reserved worldwide. www.zondervan.com The "NIV" and "New International Version" are trademarks registered in the United States Patent and Trademark Office by Biblica, Inc ™

Editor: Scott Philipp Stewart

ISBN: 9780692442166

Printed and bound in the United States of America

MAY15

BOOK OF TESTIMONIES

TEN TESTIMONIES THAT WILL CHANGE YOUR LIFE

Dr. Claire Arene-Ikedi

Acknowledgements

Many thanks to my precious son Chiedozie, Chisomebi, Joseph Ikedi, your arrival galvanized me into action and gave me the inspiration behind this book.

I really appreciate all that I have learnt over the years from attending Living Word Christian Center in Forest Park, Illinois. I have learnt a lot about taking God's Word at face value and trusting God to bring His word to pass.

I really owe Reverend Friday Ajah of Body of Christ Ministries International in Port Harcourt, River State, Nigeria a huge thank you. No words can describe all that I learnt about prayer, fasting, meditating on the word, the gifts of the Holy Spirit to mention just a few things during the years that I attended your church. A lot of that knowledge has gone into birthing this book. I am eternally grateful.

Many thanks to Mr. Kinsley Ibeh of KC Holdings Limited in Kaduna, Nigeria for all his help and support whilst completing my Youth Service in Nigeria, may God bless and reward you for your kindness.

To my sisters Kobi Emmanuella King and Julia Marke thank you for all your help and support through the years. You both have contributed to my victories during some very hard times

Finally, many thanks to my husband Dr. C. Ikedi for being a support through many tough experiences, Psalm 126: 5 -6. God is faithful.

Contents

A Poem for the Unborn 5

About the Author 7

Introduction 8

Pray When God Tells You 10

He Who Digs a Pit 13

Delivered By a Sale 18

Two Steps Ahead of Satan 26

Nothing is Too Hard for The Lord 29

You Cannot Steal My Blessing 34

God over All Delays 40

All the Glory Must Be to the Lord 45

God is My Only Source 50

Conclusion 58

A Poem for the Unborn

My darling child! Oh my darling child!

Seven weeks barely

I received news of you as a burden lifted

A new one added

With deep sobs of joy

Joy at God's honor for a woman scorned, accused, and rejected

To me you are, His arms of comfort, His love, His presence

You must be great!! My darling child to mean all this to me

My darling child! Oh my darling child!

A burden lifted, a new one added

How my darling child can I protect you from my life?

To me you are deep prayers answered

His glory that no man can claim, man's works regardless

You must be great!! My darling child to mean all this to me

Seven weeks barely!

My darling child! Oh my darling child!

To me you are the timeliness of His signs and wonders

My rainbow in the midst of a storm

My darling child! Oh my darling child!

My great honor and reward from heaven

A burden lifted, a new one added

Your life must be better my child

Full of love and laughter

My darling child! Oh my darling child!

Seven weeks barely

You must be great my child!

You started with deep prayers

Of a woman scorned, accused, and rejected

I received the news of you with deep sobs of joy

To me you are

A sign of His love, His presence, His comfort

You must be great! My darling child to mean this much to me

Seven weeks barely

Your life must be a sign!

For Joseph

©Cannot be reproduced or used in any format without the express written permission of the owner, Dr. Claire C. Arene-Ikedi

This book of testimonies is aimed at two groups—those who do not yet believe in Jesus and those who do believe and need a reminder that we serve a prayer-answering God. The beauty of a book about real-life testimonies is that there is no theme to the testimonies presented in this collection. Trials and life-challenges do not come according to any particular schedule nor do they follow a set theme. Therefore this collection of testimonies presents stories about a vast array of challenges in various areas of life. It is a book that has something for everyone.

My prayer is that this book will indeed be a prophecy of your victory in any challenging circumstance you may be facing. It is also my fervent prayer that this book will sows seeds in the hearts of those who do not yet know Jesus. Seeds that will yield the faith that ultimately leads to a relationship with Jesus. My struggles and challenges as a Christian are not yet over, but the God who has been faithful in all of the circumstances I share here will surely be faithful in everything that lies ahead. May God bless you as you read.

Pray When God Tells You

This is a true story of deliverance that happened in my life when I was 18 years old and in my first year in university. I was still very young in my faith and very active in the Christian youth ministry on campus at the time. Psalm 34:7, which says, "The angel of the Lord encamps around those who fear him and he delivers them", is the supporting scripture for this true life testimony. I was really just getting to know the Lord at this phase of my life, and this is one of the memories I have of how God worked in my life to strengthen my knowledge of Him and really let me know that His Word is true and faith in it still produces the same results in these times as it did in the days of old.

I had a very challenging childhood and had to learn very early in life how to call upon God. As a result, as a young college student I was a very prayerful Christian. One night I had stayed out late studying for an impending exam. By the time I started walking back home from the library it was almost 2:00 in the morning. I was walking home with my friend and prayer partner who was going to walk me part of the way and then head on to her hostel because she lived in the university's hostels for students whilst I lived with my father and step-mother. My father at that time was a college professor and lived on campus as did the other lecturers and professors. As my friend and I were walking home, for some reason, I started to feel a tug in my heart that I needed to stop immediately and start praying.

The urge that came upon me was so great that I told my friend, and we stopped and found a little private area where we could pray. We began to intercede in the Spirit, praying both in English and in our Heavenly tongue. I did not at the time know or understand why I was so burdened to pray, but I was glad that my friend agreed to stop and pray with me. We interrupted our journey back home for a good 15–30 minutes. After praying and expending the prayer burden, my friend left and I continued my journey back home alone.

When I got home, the first thing I noticed was that the door was wide open. At first I thought that someone at home was up but this was unlikely, given that it was almost 3 in the morning. So I proceeded to enter the house cautiously and quite afraid. What awaited me as I entered the living room was evidence that the house had been burgled; intuitively I felt that I must have just missed the burglars.

In that moment, I immediately realized why God had delayed my coming home and caused me to be so burdened with the need to pray. At that moment, rather than focus on all the valuables that had been taken from the house, I was overcome with joy and gratitude that God had counted me worthy of His protection and deliverance. I realized that if I had arrived home just a little earlier I would have fallen prey to the devil's plans for me to walk in on a burglary and possibly be harmed or, worse still, killed.

He Who Digs a Pit

This second testimony occurred when I was living in Kaduna, Nigeria, completing my national youth service, which is a mandatory 12-month program that all recent graduates from Nigerian universities have to complete in order to qualify for employment in Nigeria. I have chosen Psalm 35:8 as the supporting verse for this scripture. It says: "May ruin overtake them by surprise, may the net they hid entangle them, may they fall into the pit, to their ruin". These are strong words but uncanny in the way they capture exactly what took place in this testimony.

My service in Kaduna was my second attempt at trying to complete the program. Placements were made randomly —or rather they were *supposed to be made randomly* by government officials, and my previous placement had been in Kano, a predominantly Muslim State in northern Nigeria. It had been very difficult to serve there because I had no family support and eventually I was unable to complete my service.

This time, with the help of my father's younger brother, I was assigned to a law office owned by a lawyer who had done some work for my uncle. Although Kaduna is not as thoroughly a Muslim state as Kano, it is still *very* Muslim, especially for someone who had lived most of her life in the southern states of Nigeria, which are predominantly Christian, I felt very out of place and alone for quite a while. For some time, I walked around feeling like "I was sticking out like a sore thumb". I was very relieved therefore when one of the ladies in an adjacent office, an administrative assistant, appeared to take a liking to me and always engaged me in conversation. Before long, I was taking my lunch break to coincide with hers and I would meet her in her office where we would spend lunch time chatting and sharing the details of our lives. She was also from one of the southern states and was a "Christian", which made it even easier for me to bond and let down my guard with her. I felt like I had met a sister in a faraway land.

Soon enough, our conversations (as nearly all women's conversation tend to do) turned to the men in our lives. I was not really attached at the time, though I was interested in someone. She, on the other hand, informed me that she was engaged, and not to just anyone, but to a man who lived in England. She shared with me her plan to join him after they got married. I was excited for her and she was very excited too. She later introduced me to her fiancé over the phone on one of the days when I went over to her office for lunch. Over time, whenever I went over to her office for lunch, her fiancé would be on the phone. We would both chat with him. I didn't think anything of it. I just assumed she was very happy and proud to be engaged to someone who was eventually going to help her move abroad. In time I would realize that I was very naïve.

Our friendship continued to grow over the next few months. But then I started noticing that my boss, my uncle's lawyer friend who had given me the youth service job, started asking me a lot of questions about my family. He wanted to know where each member of my family lived and specifically if I had any family living abroad and, if so, how I kept in touch with them. Two of my sisters were living in England at that time, and my mother was living in the United States. I did not think much of his questions, even when one afternoon he asked me to call abroad so he could speak to my mother. Really! That was the strangest request ever, but I complied.

After all of these strange questions and requests, he asked me one day if I had ever used the phone in the adjacent office to call abroad—specifically to England. I told him no, of course, and stated that I called abroad regularly but always used a dialing card to do so. He then told me that the owner of the office had complained to him that I had come to his office during my lunch breaks and made international calls and had run up his phone bill to over 100,000.00 Naira, which was about $1,000 (One Thousand Dollars). By this time, of course, I had begun to realize that "my friend" had dug a really deep hole for me. I had no way of proving that I was telling the truth, because my boss told me that all of the calls had been dialed direct through the operator using *my* name. It was up to my boss; a Muslim, to give me the benefit of the doubt—and he did. He told his friend in the other office, who was also a Muslim that it was very unlikely that I had made the calls and that he should look more closely at the people in his own office. I understood then the reason behind his very strange questions about my family and his even weirder request that I call my mother so he could speak to her.

His colleague took his advice and further investigated the incident and eventually discovered that it was indeed his administrative assistant who had made all the calls dialing directly through the operator and had used my name instead of hers. She had deliberately introduced me to her fiancé and made sure I was always there when she was speaking to him so that he would remember my name just in case anyone ever called to ask him if he knew someone named Claire. To this day I do not know whether he was in on the deceit or not.

What will forever stick in my mind was a visit that my boss, his colleague, and I made to a prison. I thought it was just a routine prison visit with one of the clients my boss was representing. When we got there, however, I saw "my friend" (the one who had set me up for her long distance romance calls). She looked so frightened that I felt very sorry for her in spite of all that had happened because I would not wish incarceration in a Nigerian prison even on my worst enemy.

The Bible tells us in the book of Psalms that "whoever digs a hole and scoops it out falls into the pit they have made" (Psalm 7:15). So it was with my "friend" who ended up falling in the pit she had dug for me. Although I was completely oblivious to her plans and intentions and, in my ignorance and innocence, did absolutely nothing to protect myself, God in His kindness was faithful to His Word in Psalm 91 concerning those who trust in Him: He gave His angels charge over me and they kept me from striking my foot against the stone my "friend" had prepared for me. Glory be to God!

Delivered By a Sale

The story in this testimony occurred when I moved from Nigeria to the United States to further my education. I lived in Florida for a while initially before relocating from there to Illinois. I have chosen Psalms 25:12 and 32:8 as the supporting scriptures for this testimony. Psalm 25:12 says: "Who, then, are those who fear the LORD? He will instruct them in the ways they should choose". Psalm 32:8 says: "I will instruct you and teach you in the way you should go; I will counsel you with my loving eye on you". During the time I was in Florida, whilst still completing my master's degree, with God's help I had purchased a 1-bedroom condo. I continued to own it even after I moved to Illinois. As time passed, however, it became very difficult to continue owning properties in both Florida and Illinois. Even though the condo was being managed and rented out by a real estate agent I had great faith in and who was always faithful to collect my rent payments, it was becoming increasingly difficult after each lease ended to find reliable tenants.

Additionally, the tenants always had one thing or another that they needed fixed, and it really was becoming tedious coordinating all of those repairs from Illinois. Even the real estate management company had begun to signal that managing the property for me was becoming too much of a burden, and I knew for sure that I could not manage the property on my own if they decided to quit on me.

All of these concerns led me to decide to sell the unit. Luckily for me, the tenant I had at the time decided that he wanted to buy the unit almost as soon as I put it on the market. So almost immediately after I put it up for sale I found someone to buy it. Everything seemed to be falling in place nicely. In fact, if the sales contract went through I stood to make about three times as much as I had paid for the condo. Everything seemed to be too good to be true, however, and for some reason I just felt uneasy and reluctant to go through with the deal—so much so in fact that I tried to back out of going through with the sale on some technicality that I could have overlooked if I wanted to. The buyer refused to back out because apparently he thought he had found quite a good deal and was unwilling to give it up. So we spent some time arguing back and forth in writing and there was even talk of a lawsuit.

After much contemplation, I decided to just let go of the unit. I was angry and felt as though I was being forced to sell my home against my will, but after all the back-and-forth and threats, I also felt at peace that I was letting go. With the help of the attorney I hired to represent me in the sale, the closing went through and I made a huge profit.

Not quite a week after the closing, I received a letter from the attorney who had represented the buyer in the sale. The buyer was threatening to sue me, ostensibly because the entire ceiling of the unit had caved in. They accused me of concealing the fact that the unit was in a state of disrepair and selling the unit despite knowing that the ceiling was going to cave in.

Given the fact that I had tried to back out of the sale repeatedly and had even stalled closing on the sale for weeks (all of which was in writing between our attorneys), the buyer could not convincingly claim that I had deceitfully sold to him a property that was in a state of disrepair. Additionally, the condo had passed all inspections prior to closing, so there really wasn't much the buyer or his attorney could do once I reminded them of these facts. They stopped contacting me after a while and never filed a lawsuit.

For my part, though, I continued to reflect on what had happened. *Why had I suddenly developed cold feet about something that was so obviously a very profitable sale?* I came to the conclusion that indeed everything does happen for a reason, and in this case if I had not tried so hard to back out of the sale it was likely I would have been sued. I am certain that God, who certainly knew what was about to happen, was looking out for me. That is why things happened as they did. Interestingly, by the end of the year in which I sold the condo property values had fallen so much that I would have made much less profit on the sale if I had been successful in my attempt to back out of the sale. Indeed, as the Scriptures tell us in Romans 8:28: "And we know that in all things God works for the good of those who love him, who have been called according to his purpose".

You Are Dead Without Jesus

This testimony did not come to mind at first as one I would include in my collection of testimonies because it is not a testimony of something that God did for me. I continued to feel a tug in my heart to include it however, and as I reflected on why I came to believe that God wanted me to include it because it is a testimony of the reality of the invisible world, the reality of eternal life in which all Christians believe. I have selected Hebrews 9:27 as the supporting scripture verse for this testimony, it says "Just as people are destined to die once and after that to face judgment".

This experience occurred when I was about 18 years old. Its impact on me was to make my belief in Jesus even stronger. A certain aunt (who was related to me by marriage) had four children, two boys and two girls. The younger girl and I were very close friends. Sometime towards the end of my first year in college, my aunt became ill and was admitted to hospital. Her illness was not serious, and she was to be treated with a routine procedure and then discharged.

As is so often the case in Nigeria, however, routine procedures sometimes go awry. Anyway, my aunt's daughter gave me no sign *that* anything was wrong with her mother and thus I was completely in the dark about her admission to hospital. I suppose she probably did not let me know anything about her mom's condition because she thought it was nothing to be concerned about and could be treated with a routine surgical procedure.

I don't know how long my aunt was in hospital before this took place, but one night as I was sleeping I saw my aunt appear before me dressed in white. She seemed very cheerful in the dream, but she said to me, "I am not dead; your father is dead". At that point I woke up startled and worried in spirit. Having no idea that my aunt was even in the Hospital, my first thought about the dream was that it was a warning that my father was about to die. When I woke up that morning, however, as I was descending the stairs towards the living room, my father was sitting right there in full view. He looked so despondent that I could not help asking what the matter with him was. My dad then looked at me very sorrowfully and told me that my aunt had died very unexpectedly following a routine procedure at a renowned hospital in Nigeria.

That news came as such a surprise that I stood there stunned. I did not know what to say. I then recalled the dream from the previous night. I could not share it with my dad because of what my aunt had told me in the dream. I began to reflect on what she had said from a spiritual perspective. What I then came to understand was that my aunty was saying to me that she was alive and well even though she was physically dead. I could understand what she meant because my aunty had given her life to Christ just a few months before she took ill and was quite a changed person. On the other hand, I also understood her statement about my father's being dead to mean that my father needed to accept the message of his salvation through Jesus Christ because until he did that he was spiritually dead even though he was physically alive.

I believe that my interpretation of the dream is scripturally sound, and whenever I remember and share this story I do so because it is a constant reminder that the invisible realms of Heaven and Hell, good and evil are so real.

Although it was sad for my friend that her mother died, she and her siblings were encouraged and somewhat comforted when I shared my dream with them—especially when I shared what their mother said about her not being dead. Something else I noticed from this experience was that God is so kind that He found a way to confirm my aunt's salvation to her children since she was newly saved and they probably wondered about her eternal status. God in His kindness also found a means to comfort them about her continued and joyful existence in the invisible realm of the spirit.

This was one of the dreams that helped to solidify my commitment to living out the Christian faith and treating this world as the transient place that the Bible says it is.

Two Steps Ahead of Satan

This testimony is my account and experience of God's faithfulness in the area of protecting His servants and those who trust in Him. I have selected Psalm 91:11-12 as the supporting scripture for this testimony. It says: "For he will command his angels concerning you to guard you in all your ways; they will lift you up in their hands, so that you will not strike your foot against a stone".

Not too long ago, I had to drive about two hours daily (sometimes almost three if the traffic was bad) to work as a pre-doctoral intern sometimes in very harsh weather conditions. The pre-doctoral internship was in Milwaukee, Wisconsin. I had accepted it by faith despite its being such a great distance away because I had obtained the position through much prayer and the Holy Ghost's intervention (a story which is itself a testimony in its own right).

One morning as I was driving to Wisconsin I suddenly felt moved to prayer. It happened so suddenly, almost as though there was another presence in the car that I started to pray in the Spirit and also in my own understanding. As I recall, when I prayed in my understanding I was saying aloud that God would protect me from death by car accident and declaring angelic protection and victory over any attack of demonic forces on my safety. I also found myself reciting portions of the book of Psalms on protection and deliverance from premature death.

Not quite five minutes after I had said these prayers as I was still driving I heard a loud explosion-like sound. I was driving about 65 miles per hour. My car jerked a little and started to sound different. Not knowing what had happened, I started to slow down and looked for a safe place to pull over. At the same time I started noticing other drivers' trying to flag me down, so I found a spot and pulled over. When I got out of the car the first thing I noticed was that the rear tire on the driver's side was torn to shreds. It was at that point that I understood why the Holy Spirit had moved me towards intercession and prayer. Given the great damage to my tire and the speed I was driving, the blowout could have led to my being seriously injured or even killed.

Instead, however, I was parked on the side of the highway safe and unharmed waiting for AAA because I partake in the divine nature, which includes divine protection by God's angels. I thank God for His protection that is available to all who put their faith in Him.

Nothing is Too Hard for The Lord

This testimony is a testimony of answered prayers, divine provision, and divine direction through dreams. Many times in the Bible we see stories about how God directed His saints and those who call upon His name through dreams. One of my objectives for writing this collection of testimonies is to help everyone who reads them realize that the God who directed His saints through dreams and answered prayers 2,000 years ago has not changed one bit. He is still doing the same today, and this direction is not a special gift reserved only for pastors or priests or other "special" believers. It is available to everyone everywhere who believes in the name of the Lord Jesus. I have chosen Matthew 2:12 as the supporting verse for this testimony. It says: "And having been warned in a dream not to go back to Herod, they returned to their country by another route".

On more occasions than I can recall, God has intervened in my life or directly answered my prayers or told me what direction to take when I have been in a bind through dreams. As a result, I got into the habit of writing my dreams down. Unfortunately, I only started doing this after I learned that ignoring my dreams had caused me to make some really costly mistakes. The testimony I share here is about one of the positive outcomes of responding to my dreams.

Not too long ago, I was at a major crossroad. I had reached the final stages of my doctoral program in clinical psychology. I had been much delayed in completing my degree because I had to work throughout the program in order to meet my financial obligations and also because I got married and had to attend to some of the obligations that come with marriage. I had reached the point at which I could be expelled from the program if I did not graduate. This would have been devastating because I had taken out loans and needed to graduate to be able to increase my income so that I could afford to pay back the loans.

One of the many challenges that students in the field of clinical psychology encounter is being able to find internships and practicum training sites in a timely manner so that they can complete the program. Currently, there are many more students than training sites. Finding a training site is even more challenging for students who are married, have children, or both. This is because very often a student has to be prepared to move out of state to find an internship. I have even seen students be separated from their families for up to a year, put homes up for sale, and so forth. Mind you, internships are usually unpaid, so those years in the program when a student has to do a practicum or an internship can be a miserable time financially and otherwise.

In my case as an older student, I was married and had several financial obligations, which I had incurred prior to my decision to go back to school. I really had to rely on God Almighty for intervention and provision each internship year because even much younger students than myself with no ties or other obligations were either not finding any training sites and having to stay longer in the program at the risk of going past the completion deadlines or making less than ideal choices such as having to move out of state or settling for mediocre non-certified sites thereby jeopardizing the value of their credentials. None of these options were amenable to me, and I had to really have faith and trust God for favor.

The year I was supposed to be completing my pre-doctoral training, it really looked like my faith had failed me and I was going to have to add another year to my program. This would have put me over the time limit to complete the program since I was already very short on time (for all the reasons I mentioned earlier). I had applied to all the certified sites and had received nothing but *NO* responses. I even reconsidered and lowered my standards and applied to sites that were not yet certified but were at least in the process of applying for certification.

Despair came each time my colleagues would tell me the sites they had been accepted at—some with the highest level of certification. I was very troubled as the application year drew to a close and I still had not found anything. I continued to pray fervently and ask my church to pray for God to open a door for me.

During this time of much prayer, I had a dream in which I saw myself struggling with an obstacle. In the dream it appeared that just as I was about to lose my struggle, somehow, I narrowly had the victory and started to sing and rejoice—and singing and dancing in a dream usually signifies victory. I woke up from that dream with the same song on my lips that I was singing in the dream, and I had such an incredible anointing to sing and dance that I must have done so for an hour or more. Even though nothing changed immediately, I knew that the internship matter had been resolved, and from that day onwards I acted and spoke with confidence as though I had found a suitable training site.

Indeed, a few weeks after I had the dream I saw an advertisement for a pre-doctoral internship. Even though the position was in another state, it was still close enough that I could drive there and come home every day. I applied immediately, and just as I had seen in the dream some obstacles arose that almost prevented me from accepting the position after it was offered to me. God gave me the victory, however, and I ended up in a certified training site. In my next testimony, I will discuss these obstacles as my experience of how the enemy of God's children battles to steal any ground God gives us and even tries to steal our answered prayers. Thank God that He is the same today, yesterday, and forever.

You Cannot Steal My Blessing

This testimony is a continuation of the previous testimony. I have chosen John 10:10 as the supporting scripture for this testimony. It says: "The thief comes only to steal and kill and destroy; I have come that they may have life, and have it to the full". Even after the dream of victory that I shared and the conviction I received through it that I was eventually going to succeed in finding an internship training site and escape having to stay an additional year in the program or worse still being expelled for non-completion, I still faced some tremendous challenges. I had to be very prayerful to face these challenges, which eventually taught me more about the truth of God's divine presence and willingness to intervene in our daily affairs *if* we choose to involve Him.

After I had the dream I described in the previous testimony and found an internship, it was somewhat of a battle before I could actually start working there. During the time in which I was applying for a pre-doctoral internship and working towards my degree, I worked full time as a clinician in a residential treatment facility for adolescents and teenagers.

My plan was to continue working at the facility if I was unable to find a suitable training site. It was not an easy place to work. The patients/clients were extremely challenging to work with, as some suffered from severe psychiatric and emotional disorders and were physically aggressive and verbally abusive towards staff. I was really hoping that I would find an internship at a training site so I could resign.

Unfortunately, however, during the time that I was awaiting a response to my application and fervently hoping that things worked out, I started to face even more difficulties at work—difficulties that were serious enough to lead me to tender my resignation to my boss and his superior. Surprisingly, they refused to accept my resignation and pleaded with me to stay. As it turned out, I should not have second-guessed my decision to leave. But I did and agreed to stay with the agency at least until I found an internship site.

I had already begun negotiating with the site that I responded to after I had the dream. Thus, as I was agreeing to put off resigning, I informed my bosses that I was exploring a few internship prospects. I also promised them that I would give them sufficient notice when I accepted an offer and vowed to help train my replacement to the extent possible. After this discussion it was my understanding that I would be staying on at the agency at least until I found an internship. Thus, I assumed that I still had my full-time job. Although I desperately wanted to find a training site, I at least had the job to help me hold out in the event that the training sites I was considering were not suited to my needs.

At this time I was almost three months past the deadline for beginning my training, and I was in serious negotiations with a particular agency that eventually offered me a spot in their training program. On the other hand, I had some concerns and went back and forth for many days because this training site was still in the process of obtaining accreditation/certification and was also some distance away (though I would still be much better off than other students who had to move to another state). Another obstacle was that my school did not approve of the site since it had not yet obtained full certification. If I accepted this training site I would literally be on my own and the school would bear no responsibility if things went awry. The training director at my school was very reluctant to grant me approval to accept this site.

After much prayer, and with further caution from the training director about accepting a site without full accreditation, I emailed the training program and informed them that I would not be joining their program as a pre-doctoral intern. I was soon to find out what a trap the enemy had set for me.

I sent the email out to the training site in the morning, and, believe it or not, no sooner had I sent it out than I noticed that I had missed a voicemail from the training director at my school. In the voicemail she said that I could go ahead and accept the training site's offer, provided that I had done my due diligence to assess the quality of the training and was comfortable with the fact that it was not an accredited site.

Missing that voicemail was only the beginning of the enemy's attempt to rob me of God's answered prayer. Later that afternoon, my boss called me into his office for what I thought was a routine discussion. After some preliminary niceties, however, he informed me that they would like me to go ahead and tender my resignation. I was not quite sure what he meant, so I tried to clarify it. Was he firing me? He said, "No", but then repeated that he would like me to go ahead and resign because in fact he had already hired someone else to fill my position. I was dumbfounded by the duplicity and struggled to keep my cool as I reminded him of what I thought was the understanding we had and asked him why he had given me the impression that he wanted me to stay on.

By the time I left my boss's office, I was really numb. I simply could not understand why anyone would behave that way, and I was also struggling to come to terms with the mess I was in. I had rejected a potential training site—in fact, the *only* training site that I had been in serious negotiations with, thereby guaranteeing that I would exceed the allotted time for completing my degree. This put me at risk of expulsion from the program. And, as if all that was not bad enough, I had been asked to resign from my job. I was just in a daze at the sheer magnitude of the mess I was in.

I began to do the only thing I knew how to do—pray, and very fervently, too. At some point, I decided to reach out to the training site again to let them know that I would be willing to join their pre-doctoral program with the assurance that they would obtain complete certification so that the quality and marketability of my degree would not be compromised. Even though I was really desperate at this point, I was still not willing to settle. As God would have it, they were still interested in me despite my previous rejection of their offer. They assured me that they were committed to becoming a fully credentialed site and indicated that they were still willing to offer me a position. In my mind, this had to be God because at the time these things were happening any site that still had an opening probably had more interested pre-doctoral students willing to fill the spot than they could handle. That they would accept me back when I had rejected their initial offer and was giving them conditions *had* to be God.

I went on to resign from my job—not when they requested but a few days before my internship began. The internship site also obtained full accreditation a few months after I started my internship. The accreditation came early enough for my entire training experience to be certified at an accredited training site. Only God in His faithfulness could have delivered me from all those traps the enemy set for me so He could stifle my blessings and further delay my life. Indeed God delivered me from the snare of the fowler.

God over All Delays

This testimony occurred over a period of about nine years. It is not unlike the Lord to take His time to manifest His presence and His victory over the enemy's ploys. Oftentimes, when Christians go through fire it is not so much that the Lord is chastising them as it is that He is molding their faith and giving them the spiritual understanding necessary for lasting victory. In my case the testimony that I share in this section is a culmination of events that unfolded before my eyes over a period of nine years. Now, upon reflection, I can see God's help and intervention in every detail although at the time I could not see what I see now. I have chosen Psalm 113:9 as the supporting verse for this testimony. It says: "He settles the childless woman in her home as a happy mother of children. Praise the LORD".

Not quite two months after I got married, I started to experience a continuous and nagging pain in my abdominal area. For a while I tried to ignore it. After a while, though, I could no longer ignore it and felt it was wise to try to find out what was causing the pain. At the doctor's visit, they performed an ultrasound, and after reviewing the results the physician told me that I had fibroids that were at that time still manageable. Since I was already in my early thirties and not yet a biological mom, she advised that I begin to think seriously about having a child because the fibroids could potentially grow so large and make it difficult either to conceive or to carry a child to term, risking the child's well-being and also creating complications during the pregnancy. I took the doctor's counsel to heart and was intending to reorganize my priorities so that I could begin raising a family. Subsequent events proved to me that God had a plan and that the enemy had a plan as well.

At that time, however, I was in a marriage that I did not want to bring a child into because it was an unsafe and unhealthy relationship—all of which I had discovered out soon after the marriage. I remember praying to God and letting Him know that I truly desired a child but that if my marriage was not destined to work out I also did not want to bring a child into the world into a broken home. This is not to say that mothers who do this are not loved by God or not good mothers, but I had so little support and just didn't think I would be able to cope. It was not long after I said these prayers that the marriage completely went downhill due to my safety being threatened and eventually came to an end. It was a devastating time for me and also a very fearful time because here I was losing my husband and suffering from a medical condition that meant the window of childbearing was closing—the doctor had told me I had to act fast or possibly end up having a very difficult time trying to conceive or not being able to conceive at all.

After the divorce, and as the years went by, I watched as the fibroids grew larger and larger despite much prayer until it got to the point when the doctors told me I had to have them taken out or risk having to get a hysterectomy and losing the ability ever to conceive a child. At the time the doctors told me this, I could not have had the surgery despite my desire to be rid of the fibroids because I had changed insurance. My insurance at the time would not have paid for a surgery that was over $30,000 because my condition was ruled "a pre-existing condition". I never despaired or became desperate, however. Instead, I stood my ground in both confession and prayer. In fact when I finally began to date seriously again, almost nine years after my divorce, and eventually got engaged, I remember my fiancé encouraging me to marry him quickly so that I could be put on his insurance and get the surgery done. However, I resisted every pressure to do so because the last thing I wanted was any man to take the glory for my healing. By this time, the fibroid tumors were so large that I looked like I was eight months pregnant and constantly had people asking me when the baby was due. I even had some Christian friends who should have known better spreading rumors that I was pregnant out of wedlock. I had already started experiencing symptoms such as fluid retention in my lower extremities and I was frequently in a lot of pain.

I continued to intercede and ask other Christians and the church to intercede for me. As the prayers intensified, I started to have dreams of victory and in fact had a number of dreams in which I saw myself the mother of children and other dreams in which I saw myself successfully treated with surgery. Not long after these dreams, God made me aware of a hospital program for people who needed surgery but could not afford it or were uninsured. I applied and received approval almost immediately to have the entire—I repeat, the entire—expense of my surgery, all $30,000-plus of it, written off by the hospital.

My symptoms were getting quite severe at the time, so I scheduled the surgery immediately after my application was approved. The surgery was very successful. In fact, God showed up again because the doctor had wanted to use a very powerful drug to prevent the possibility that I could bleed profusely, but because one of the side-effects of this drug was that it could cause me to go into menopause I refused it. In spite of my refusal of the recommended drug, everything went well.

As I write this, I am married and the extremely happy and amazed mother of a baby boy. His arrival is a testimony that I share in another testimony in this book of testimonies. "He settles the childless woman in her home as a happy mother of children. Praise the LORD" (Psalm 113:9).

All the Glory Must Be to the Lord

One thing I believe is that God *always* finds a way to strengthen the faith of those who trust in Him. Thus, even when we accomplish things seemingly through natural means, God finds a way to let us know that even natural things would not work if His favor were not on it. One thing that the testimony I am sharing here taught me is that God can and does manifest Himself and answer prayers even through natural means and media. I have chosen 2 Kings 20:7 as the supporting scripture for this testimony. It says: "Then Isaiah said, 'Prepare a poultice of figs. They did so and applied it to the boil, and he recovered".

After my fibroid removal surgery, it was still a battle of faith to see my desire to have biological children fulfilled. At this time I was about 40 years old and remarried. Although the surgery was very successful, I was not getting pregnant. All the doctors we consulted with said that besides possibly the effect of age, there was no reason why my husband and I were not conceiving. The doctors recommended fertility treatments and again urged me to move fast to prevent the possibility of having a baby with a genetic disorder or the likelihood that even fertility treatments would not be effective owing to my age.

I struggled for a very long time with the ethics of submitting to fertility treatments and even wondered if it was even a sound spiritual choice. To be quite sincere, I had also gone through these same struggles prior to my surgery because all my life I had heard that God heals people supernaturally. Thus, I struggled with why I was not getting healed supernaturally and why I had to submit to fertility treatments rather than being able to conceive naturally like everyone else.

Because of these internal struggles I delayed fertility treatments for about two and a half years as I was holding out in prayer believing that God would help me conceive. Throughout this time, I kept on remembering some scriptures that had come to me before my surgery. One of the scriptures was the story about how Jesus healed a blind man by mixing some dust and spit and putting it in his eyes. To me that was evidence of God's healing supernaturally through the use of a natural medium. The second scripture was the incident in the Old Testament when the Prophet Elisha healed King Hezekiah of a disease by using a medicinal concoction that he instructed him to put on his body. The healing was supernatural because it was spoken about prophetically before it actually occurred. Before it actually came to be, however, a natural medium was involved.

Obviously, there are many instances of healing in the Bible that did not involve any natural media or means, but in these scriptural instances I have cited something natural was used as a route for the manifestation of healing.

As I prayed about this and thought about these scriptures for a while, I became increasingly comfortable with submitting to the procedures and fertility treatments the doctors recommended. By this time, however, I had waited so long that the doctor was no longer recommending that procedure or that particular fertility treatment but something more intense because at my age it was considered a waste of time to do the procedure the doctor had previously recommended. In fact, it had only a 10% chance of success for women my age. The 10% who succeeded usually did not succeed on the first try but only after several tries. In fact, this particular procedure was not allowed at all for women my age in other countries. For instance, it would not have been permitted if I was in Great Britain.

I was, however, completely opposed to undergoing the more intensive and invasive treatment my doctor was recommending at this time. So I began to pray, and two scriptures came to my mind: Psalm 113:11 – "He settles the childless woman in her home as a happy mother of children. Praise the LORD", and Psalm 92:12 - 14 – "The righteous will flourish like a palm tree, they will grow like a cedar of Lebanon; planted in the house of the Lord, they will flourish in the courts of our God. They will still bear fruit in old age, they will stay fresh and green. I had instructions not only to fast and pray but also to join with my husband in confessing these scriptures daily for 30 days. With renewed confidence and no longer feeling so conflicted, my husband and I fasted and prayed and confessed those scriptures every day for 30 days before we started the treatments.

I want to report that today as I write this book of testimonies the treatment was successful and on the first try. I did not have to do the more invasive treatment. I got pregnant after the first round of treatment with fertility hormones to help me ovulate and release more eggs. My healthy and very happy baby boy was born when I was a few months shy of my 43rd birthday. My non-Christian doctor called him a miracle baby. Answered prayers and faith accomplished what they are supposed to do—they drew attention to God and to the supernatural. To God be all the glory.

God is My Only Source

The testimony I share here is so germane to what some children all over the world have experienced in their childhood. I have chosen Psalm 27:10 as the supporting scripture for this testimony. It says: "Though my father and mother forsake me, the LORD will receive me". This testimony proves the truth of God's Word in Psalm 27:10 and the integrity of His promises.

As a child and well into young adulthood, when I was still somewhat dependent on my parents at least financially, I was severely neglected and abused physically, verbally, and emotionally. I strongly believe that a saving grace for me was that I came to know the Lord Jesus as my personal savior when I was about 16 years old. I believe this is the sole reason I have been able to thrive and achieve some measure of success with my life in spite of the hardships I endured at the hands of my father and his wife, my step-mother.

These hardships included neglecting to provide for my material needs (for example, for clothing) in an equitable manner although my half-brothers and sisters had their needs met. I was denied food to the point that my physical growth was affected as I was extremely underweight and malnourished. They used severe physical and corporal punishment to the point that I often had scars on my body. I could go on and on about all I suffered at the hands of my father and his wife, but I want to say that these things make it all the more amazing and glorious that I am here today and not just here but strong.

The effect of all the abuse and neglect I suffered as a child was that I had to learn at a very young age, and early on in my walk with Christ, how to pray until I got an answer and how to trust the Lord for my needs. I never had what other children had, but it was always a testimony of God's reality and presence in my life that He always found a way to provide me with things that my parents ought to have given me, sometimes abundantly and in a way that made me know it was God the Father providing for me.

This was the story of my experience of God when I was in Kaduna, Nigeria, completing my youth service, which is a program that all individuals have to complete before they are eligible for employment. In this phase, graduates often still have to rely on their parents for sustenance because youth service positions are like volunteer work and often pay so little that they are not enough for survival or self-sustenance. Indeed, such was my experience during my youth service training. I could not afford to pay for food, clothing, or shelter.

During that one-year of community service, however, God continually connected me with some of the wealthiest people in Nigeria. Only God could have brought me before some of the top people in government and business and caused me to find favor to the point that I was regularly gifted. Though I did absolutely nothing to solicit or ask for anything, I was regularly receiving extra money beyond the pittance that I was paid as a youth service employee that I could not possibly live off of. But for God's kindness through these people who helped me I would have starved or had to resort to begging or criminal or immoral behavior because the entire time I spent in youth service neither my father nor his wife sent me a cent, although they knew very well that I was not making enough at that point to be self-sustaining.

Out of this overflow of generosity I was able to complete all the necessary steps and pay all the costs associated with obtaining a travel visa and even pay for my own ticket after my youth service was completed. And all this without receiving even one cent from my father and his wife, though later on my half-sisters and brothers travelled abroad regularly. In my case, God found a way to supply my needs according to His riches in glory by Christ Jesus when Satan had planned for me to be forsaken. Indeed, it is my testimony that I was so well taken care of during my youth service year that I lived much better than some of my colleagues who had wealthy caring parents. To God be the glory!

I would like anyone reading this testimony to know that these things did not happen by chance or coincidence. Knowing the kind of family I came from and that I would have no support during my youth service year, I had prayed much prior to setting out to begin the program. I remember giving a tithe of about 10,000 Niara (which in these times would translate to about $100) to the man of God in whose church I worshipped from the very limited funds I had at the time. I remember that he prayed with me and pronounced blessings on my stay in Kaduna. By the time the year was completed, I had seen all those blessings come to pass and had received in cash and kind more than a hundred times what I had sown in faith and in tears. To God be the glory!

In the mid-1990s I moved to the United States to continue my education and reconnect with my biological mother from whom I had been separated since I was a toddler. I had been looking forward to this time for many, many years. Many surprises, disappointments, and unforeseen circumstances were awaiting me. This testimony is about how God saw me through the experiences I had during my first year living in the United States.

As I said, my two-fold intention in moving was to continue my education and to reconnect with my biological mother. It turns out that my mother had totally different ideas about why she had showed interest in my coming over to the United States. I had planned to stay with my mother while I continued my studies at a nearby university. Soon enough, though, I discovered that my mother had invited me over because she needed help with setting up a business and had hoped that I would help financially and also do the necessary leg work to get the business started. When I made it clear that I really wanted to focus on furthering my education and had no intention of giving her what little money I was making selling train tickets for children's train rides at the mall, she eventually kicked me out of her house.

It was a very depressing time for me because I had thought that she, having not been in my life since I was little more than a toddler, was as excited as I was to reconnect with her and establish a relationship. When this turned out not to be her motive for wanting me to come over, it took me a while to wrap my mind around this and deal with the fact that she did not have any motherly feelings towards me. I had created all these very high hopes and big ideas about how we would make up for lost time.

I had to deal with the fact that I had come all this way for nothing and was homeless and dependent on the good graces of friends and relatives. In spite of these circumstances, my resolve to succeed was very strong because I had seen my faith work in other situations in which I had faced extreme hardship before coming to the United States. It was a challenge, however, because with a job that paid only $5 an hour in those days, I did not have enough money to afford a place of my own. So I stayed with an uncle for a few months and then lived with a family I had met in church for a short while, paying them $200 a month and helping with chores.

These were very hard times for me, and it took all the faith I had not to become despondent.

Things started to turn around for me when I was able to secure a substitute teaching certificate and a better-paying position. By the end of the year in which my mother said I could no longer stay with her, I had found my own apartment.

God's intervention was even more obvious when the Jewish man who had been renting the condominium to me informed me through his real estate representative that he was getting rid of some of his properties and would like to sell my condominium if I was interested in buying. I did not have "owning property" as one of the goals I had in mind for myself at that age, but apparently the owner had purchased the unit for peanuts and had made so much on the value that he was selling it for far less than what it was worth. Thus, it would have been absolutely stupid not to buy it. It was almost as though God was reaching down from Heaven saying, "Here is some compensation for all your troubles".

So I bought the unit and became the proud owner of my own home in my early twenties, less than two years after I had been homeless and squatting with relatives and friends. I later sold that unit for about three times what I paid for it. Indeed, God compensated me for all my troubles.

He is indeed faithful and *never ever forsakes* His children.

Conclusion

Quite frankly these testimonies are just a few of the innumerable answers to prayers, divine interventions, and outright miracles I have personally experienced or witnessed since committing my life to Christ.

It is my hope, however, that this collection of testimonies touches the hearts of all who may be in a situation in which they are struggling with doubt or perhaps not even convinced that God truly cares enough about us humans to actually intervene in our affairs.

My hope is that each of the testimonies I have shared here reveals some specific principles about getting prayers answered. I also hope that in my bid to make this book as factual as possible I have not deemphasized the fact that my journey from each challenge to victorious testimony involved frequent, if not daily, reading and meditation on scriptures from the Bible as well as much prayer, all based on the foundation of faith in the name of Jesus.

Oftentimes Christians and non-Christians express doubt in the effectiveness of prayer, especially when dealing with difficult situations. I hope that all who struggle with doubting the efficacy of prayer will have some insight into how to get their prayers answered when they read this book of testimonies.

God truly does answer prayers!!!

If this book has blessed you or stirred up your faith in Jesus, or if you have any comments or feedback, or if you would like to request copies for an outreach event please send your comments by e-mail to

Claire.ikedi@gmail.com

This is also the contact information for speaking engagements.

Thank you and be blessed

Printed in Dunstable, United Kingdom